D0230111

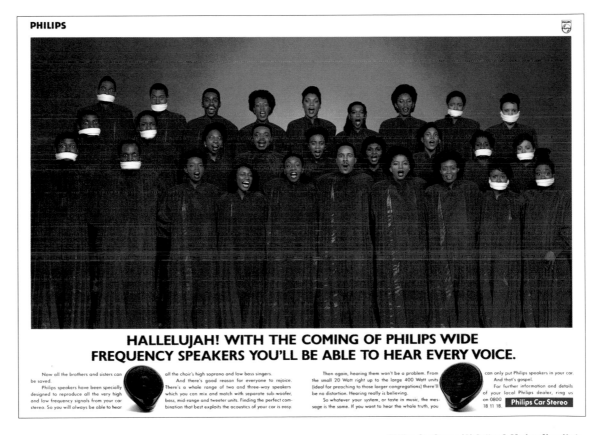

Philips Car Stereo (A) Ogilvy & Mather, New York
(AD) Brian Fraser (P) Terence Donovan

BEST ADS HUMOUR IN ADVERTISING

Dave Saunders

Smirnoff (A) Lowe Howard-Spink, London
(AD) Jeff Curtis (CW) Adrian Lim (P) Alex Buckingham

B.T. Batsford Ltd, London

To the memory of Terence Donovan and his inspiring mix of professionalism and humour

© **Dave Saunders 1997**
First published 1997
All rights reserved. No part of this publication may be reproduced
in any form or by any means without permission from the Publisher.

Printed by

for the publishers
B.T.Batsford Ltd
583 Fulham Road
London SW6 5BY

ISBN 0 7134 81056

A CIP catalogue record for this book is available from the British Library

(A) Agency, (CD) Creative Director, (AD) Art Director, (CW) Copywriter, (P) Photographer, (M) Model

CONTENTS

INTRODUCTION

Make us laugh, make us buy

Humour is one of advertising's most volatile tools. Good humour wins friends. It attracts the eye, engages the mind and restores the soul. By lowering resistance towards the product, it teases out a reaction and increases the feelgood factor. Yet humour is surrounded by banana skins. It can try too hard and fall flat. Or not hard enough and go unnoticed.

To make matters more treacherous, humour's target is a moving one. Human tastes are both varied and fickle, and, in the case of the esoteric idioms of our increasingly fragmented subcultures, very narrow and specific. Failure to understand either the product or the language of its market will relegate the advertising to oblivion – or worse – harm the product.

Since the harmless humour of the 1938 'My Goodness, My Guinness' cartoon, advertising has evolved along numerous divergent paths, exploring different applications and different vernaculars from crude slapstick to tongue-in-cheek irony. Besides establishing a rapport with the audience by inviting them to share a joke, humour can be used as a licence to address sensitive subjects, a means to bypass advertising restrictions or a weapon to combat the petty and bombastic. Although not obvious candidates for frivolous treatment, money, religion and sex - thanks to an increasingly defiant attitude towards previously taboo subjects – are now prime targets for advertisers' disarming wit. By definition, cutting edge humour breaks rules – which either offends or amuses. The acceptability of such deviance lies with the consumer. Ads that make us laugh might just make us buy.

Reprinted with kind permission of Guinness Brewing
Worldwide Ltd (A) S.H. Benson (Illustrator) John Gilroy

Funny Ha Ha

Bad hair day?!

You're a virgin, you've just given birth and now three kings have shown up.

Find out the happy ending at a church near you.

The Churches Advertising Network
(A) Christians In Media (CIM), London
(ADs/CWs) Chas Bayfield/Martin
Casson/Nick Drummond/Trevor Webb
(Illustrator) Melvyn Evans

Those who cling to a crusty image of the church say 'There's no room in the church for humour.' Everyone else sees it as a breath of fresh air that is trying to blow through the cobwebs.

**Wella Pacific Beauty Care (A) The Ball Partnership, Singapore
(CD) Robert Speechley (AD/CW) Neil French (P) Willie Tang**

We can't call the product a hair restorer, so we'll just say
'You too could have a bad hair day.'

(Be careful with the Kaminomoto)

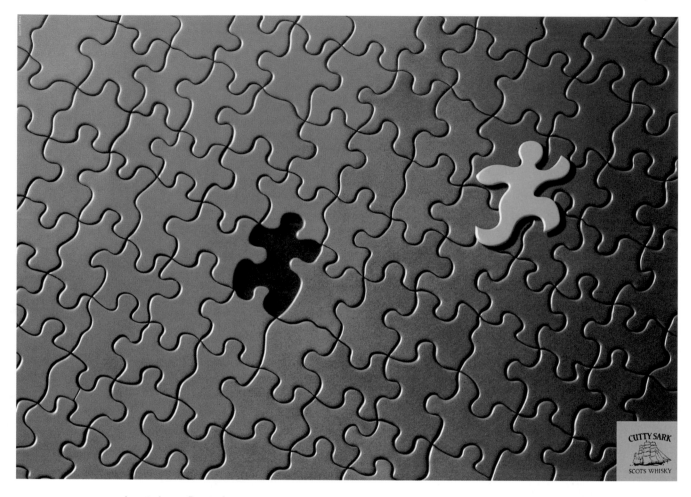

**Importaciones y Exportaciones
Varma/Cutty Sark (A) Delvico Bates, Madrid
(CDs) Pedro Soler/Enrique Astuy
(AD/CW) Angel Villalba/Jorge
Herrera/Sandra Garcia (P) Miguel Martínez**

Mates Condoms (A) Knight Leach Delaney, London (AD) Andy Wray (CW) Paul Delaney (P) John Wallace (Modelmaker) Kent & Shaw

A lot more fun than the ominous death threats of most safe sex ads.

**Expressen Newspaper (A) Alinder & Co,
Stockholm (CD) Mats Alinder (P) Lars Nyberg**

Expressen has a grip on the vital points of
life. The newspaper assumes a humorous,
yet caring attitude, while also exposing
the dirty tricks of the sly and mighty.

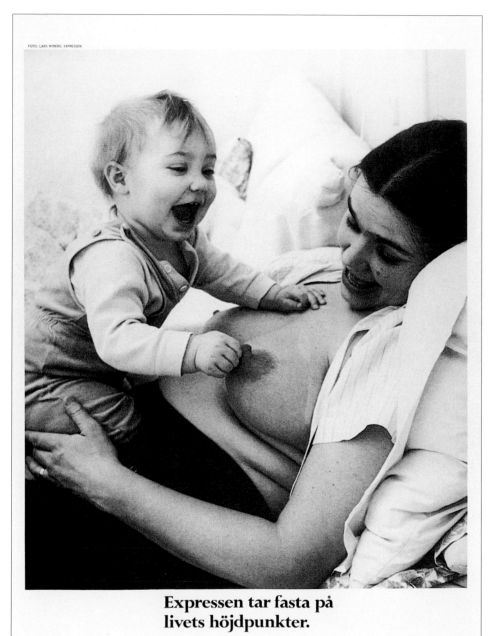

**Expressen tar fasta på
livets höjdpunkter.**

Olympus Cameras (A) Collett Dickenson
Pearce, London (P) Elliott Erwitt/Magnum

Adelaide ZOO (A) Young & Rubicam,
Adelaide (CD) Mark Lees (AD) Robyn Watt
(CW) John Warburton (P) Simon Harsent

It's party time at the Zoo.

Lincoln Park Zoo (A) Leo Burnett, Chicago

**Autan (A) Tiempo/ BBDO, Barcelona
(CW) Siscu Molina**

A brief from a client can be a licence to
have fun. But it's serious fun, because of
a commitment to the product, on which
future commissions depend.

THE HISTORY OF FLIGHT.

FROM MAN'S FIRST FRANTIC FLAPPINGS TO THE ARRIVAL OF THE JET AGE.
WITH ALL THE UPS AND DOWNS IN BETWEEN. SEE IT ALL (AND EVEN LEARN TO FLY YOURSELF)
WHEN YOU VISIT THE FLIGHT GALLERY.

**Science Museum (A) Simons Palmer
Clemmow & Johnson, London**

Make 'em smile, and you've won 'em over.

Funny Peculiar

Wampole (A) Holmes Donin Alloul, Toronto (AD) Brenda Van-Ginkle (AD/CW) Peter Holmes (P) George Simhoni

Humour is dangerous territory that works differently in different cultures and sub-cultures. As it often operates close to the edge of acceptability and respectability, it usually offends someone.

A C Barr/Irn-Bru (A) The Leith Agency,
Edinburgh (AD) Gareth Howells
(CW) Dougal Wilson (P) Ewan Myles

One man's joke is another man's
politically incorrect affront.

8 TUV | 4 GHI | 7 PRS = Truly **H**andsome **P**otato

Remember the new area code. *Ameritech.*

8 TUV | 4 GHI | 7 PRS = Tremendously **H**airy **S**cotsman

Remember the new area code. *Ameritech.*

Ameritech (A) Fallon McElligott, Minneapolis
(AD) Mike Fetrow (CW) Peter McHugh (P) Nick Vedros

Commit something to memory by inventing a
ridiculous visual association.

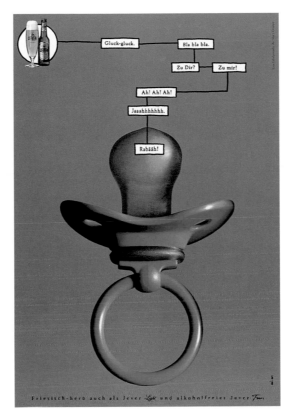

**Bavaria St. Pauli-Brauerei AG/Jever Pilsener
(A) Jung von Matt, Hamburg (CD) Deneke von
Weltzien (AD) Kai Zastrow (CW) Oliver Voss
(P) S. Putfarcken**

Your place or mine? You're as helpless as a
baby after a sip of the hard stuff.

**Central Office of Information
(A) GGT, London (AD) Erik Kessles
(CW) Johan Kramer (P) Simon Larbalestier**

This Mandrill has a good nose for
scratching records, which led to a big
contract in the music business. As you
are not similarly equipped, you'd better
sign up for a training course.

**Whitbread/Tooheys (A) Bartle Bogle
Hegarty, London (CD) John Hegarty
(AD) Russell Ramsey (CW) John O'Keeffe
(Typographer) Andy Bird**

In Australia it is now cool to have a
convict heritage, so, when relaunching
the brand as a designer lager, the
creatives drew on the brand's pedigree.

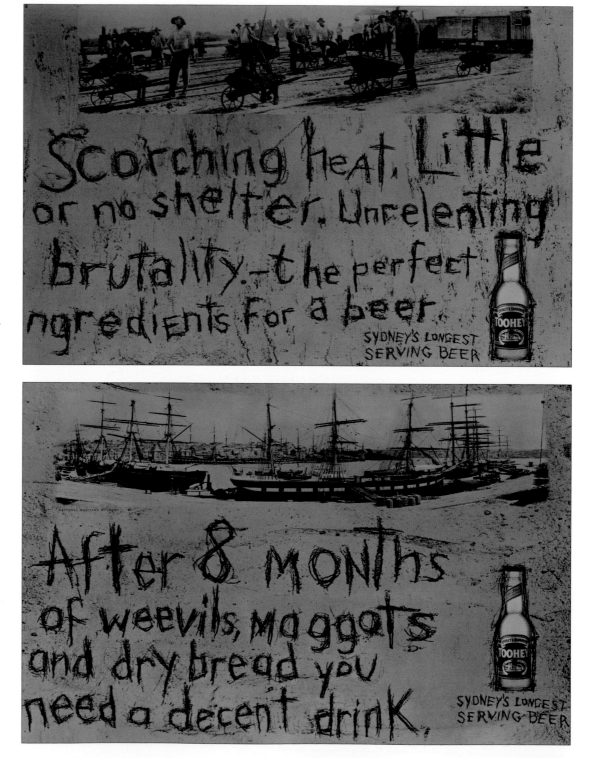

Four electric windows.

Sporty front seats.

Central locking.

Driver's airbag.

Optional four-speaker radio.

Metallic paint or flash red.

Manual air conditioning.

Electronic engine immobilizing alarm.

Alloy wheels

We didn't want to distract you.

Golf GT Special You can tell at once the new Golf GT Special is a special Golf. First of all, it's a Golf: safe, reliable and attractive. Secondly, it's a Golf GT, that is to say sprint and performan-

ce of the sports GT par excellence.

Moreover, as you can see from the picture, it has everything you can expect in a Golf, included in the price of a Golf. In addition to that, the new Golf GT Special comes in two

different engines: 1.6-litre GT 101bhp with a standard trip computer and 1.9-litre GTD 90bhp of sheer power and amazing performance, to thrill diesel enthusiasts.

Lastly, to make it even more spe-

cial, you can also ask for ABS, leather interior and electric sunroof.

In short, if we had shown you the Golf GT Special, would you have ever read all there is in the Golf GT Special?

Autogerma S.p.A./Volkswagen Golf GT Special (A) Verba DDB, Milan (CDs) Gianfranco Marabelli & Enrico Bonomini (AD) Laura Trovalusci (CW) Sofia Ambrosini (P) Carlo Paggiarino

VW was always good at breaking the mould of predictable advertising. True to the self-deprecating personality heralded by Bill Bernbach in the 1960s, the car itself is torn off the page, and - in order to find out why - you are more likely to read the copy.

I Laugh, You Cry

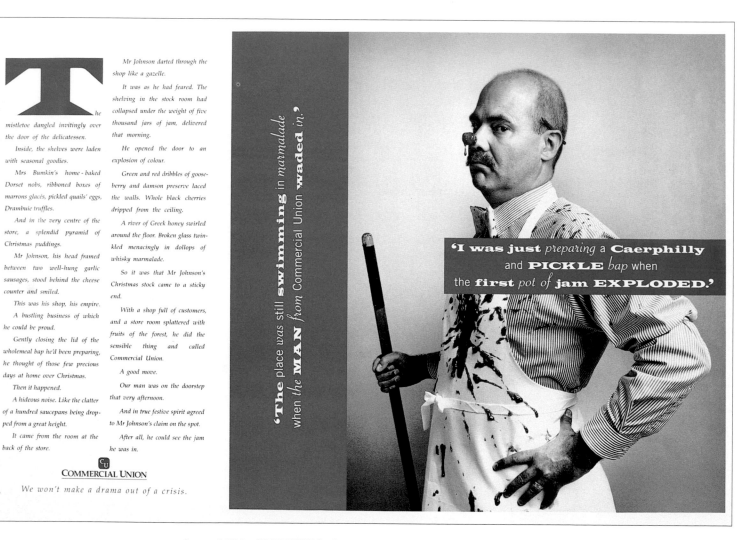

The mistletoe dangled invitingly over the door of the delicatessen.

Inside, the shelves were laden with seasonal goodies.

Mrs Bumkin's home-baked Dorset nobs, ribboned boxes of marrons glacés, pickled quails' eggs, Drambuie truffles.

And in the very centre of the store, a splendid pyramid of Christmas puddings.

Mr Johnson, his head framed between two well-hung garlic sausages, stood behind the cheese counter and smiled.

This was his shop, his empire.

A bustling business of which he could be proud.

Gently closing the lid of the wholemeal bap he'd been preparing, he thought of those few precious days at home over Christmas.

Then it happened.

A hideous noise. Like the clatter of a hundred saucepans being dropped from a great height.

It came from the room at the back of the store.

Mr Johnson darted through the shop like a gazelle.

It was as he had feared. The shelving in the stock room had collapsed under the weight of five thousand jars of jam, delivered that morning.

He opened the door to an explosion of colour.

Green and red dribbles of gooseberry and damson preserve laced the walls. Whole black cherries dripped from the ceiling.

A river of Greek honey swirled around the floor. Broken glass twinkled menacingly in dollops of whisky marmalade.

So it was that Mr Johnson's Christmas stock came to a sticky end.

With a shop full of customers, and a store room splattered with fruits of the forest, he did the sensible thing and called Commercial Union.

A good move.

Our man was on the doorstep that very afternoon.

And in true festive spirit agreed to Mr Johnson's claim on the spot.

After all, he could see the jam he was in.

COMMERCIAL UNION

We won't make a drama out of a crisis.

'The place was still **swimming** in marmalade when the **MAN** *from* Commercial Union *waded in.*'

'I was just *preparing* a **Caerphilly** and **PICKLE** *bap* when the **first** *pot of* **jam EXPLODED.**'

Commercial Union (A) CME-KHBB, London
(CD) Barbara Nokes (AD) Gary Denham
(CW) Susie Henry (P) Malcolm Venville
(Typographer) Gavin Ferguson

Of course it's not funny. Not funny at all.
Just a little crisis. No drama.

Make **sure** you're **wearing** this before **shouting** "**hi, sissies**" in a **karate** club.

Gladiator-Hi

If **you need** to run, wear **DHARMA**
DISPARADO

Dharma (A) F/Nazca Saatchi & Saatchi, Sao Paulo (CD) Fabio Fernandez

No, these shoes are not an insurance against looking uncool. They are the business when you need to move fast.

Collingwood Triathlon (A) Two Cities Advertising, Toronto (AD) Frank Lepre (CW) Judy John (P) Chris Gordaneer

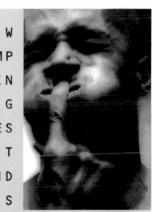

YOU KNOW THAT CRAMP YOU GET IN YOUR LEG THAT WAKES YOU UP AT NIGHT AND MAKES YOU SWALLOW YOUR PILLOW TO SUPPRESS THE SCREAM? WELL, NOW YOU CAN HAVE IT DURING THE DAY.

Super Sprint Race

THE THIRD ANNUAL COLLINGWOOD TRIATHLON JULY 23 AND 24

ScotRail (A) DMP DDB Needham, London
(AD) Mark Reddy (CW) Richard Grisdale
(P) Russell Porcas

BR.

BRRRR.

ScotRail

**Crop Marks (A) Dr Art, Toronto (AD) Doug Robinson
(CWs) Andy Manson/Tom Goudie (P) Chris Gordaneer**

Top marks Crop Marks.

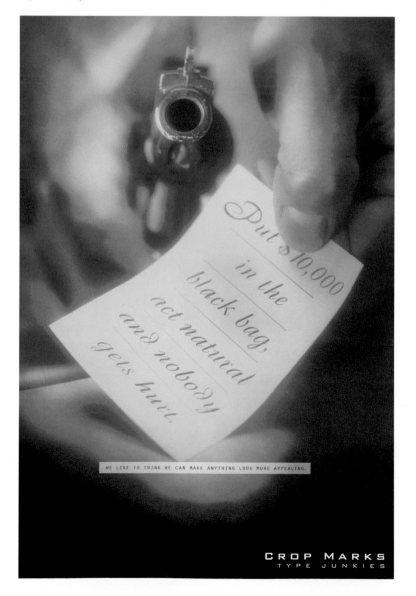

Choose our brand
or the silk
gets it.

PROTECT CHILDREN: DON'T MAKE   THEM BREATHE YOUR SMOKE

Chief Medical   Officers' Warning
5 mg Tar   0.5 mg Nicotine

**Gallaher/Silk Cut (A) M & C Saatchi,
London (AD) Carlos (CW) Keith Bickel
(P) Craig Cutler**

The rest of the story chuckles away
in our imaginations

Gallaher/Hamlet (A) Collett Dickenson Pearce, London
(CDs) Guy Moore & Tony Malcolm
(AD) Tim Brookes (CW) Ben Priest
(P) Paul Bevitt (Modelmaker) Ron Mueck

Action Man finds he is ill-equipped for
this brand of action. For him, a penis is a cigar
called Hamlet. How's that for phallic substitution?
Surely not a covert reference to the alleged link
between smoking and impotency?

TUESDAY NIGHT IS LADIES NIGHT.

BURNSVILLE PISTOL RANGE

Burnsville Pistol Range
(A) Fallon McElligott, Minneapolis
(AD) Joe Paprocki (CW) Dave Puller
(Illustrator) Bob Blewett

This simplest of adaptations creates a new target for a dormant gender consensus.

Sexual Innuendo

Playtex/Wonderbra (A) Hunt Lascaris TBWA,
Cape Town (CD) Stefania Ianigro (AD) Rui Alves
(CW) George Lesar (P) Ellen von Unwerth

Why are we so preoccupied with sex?
I blame it on hormones.

**Playtex/Wonderbra (A) Hunt Lascaris TBWA,
Cape Town (CD) Sandra de Wilt
(AD) Kirsten Hohls (CW) Desiree Brown**

Bamboo Lingerie takes a similar angle in an ad by Kirshenbaum Bond and Partners in New York. Stencilled on the pavement near the lingerie shop are the words 'From here it looks like you could use some new underwear'.

The Edinburgh Club/ The Ladies Club
(A) The Leith Agency, Edinburgh
(AD) Guy Gumm (CW) Gerry Farrell

Sexual humour crosses cultural borders well, but word play often doesn't. 'Spending a penny' is an English euphemism for going to the toilet. Although using the facilities no longer costs a penny, the term has passed into the vernacular.

Visit the Ladies without spending a penny.

THE LADIES CLUB

Come along to The Ladies Club, 15/17 Windsor Street Lane, Edinburgh, this Saturday or Sunday from 2-5 pm and take our exercise equipment for a free test drive. If you join the same day we'll give you a discount. For more information, give us a ring on 0131 558 9200.

**Gallaher/Silk Cut (A) M & C Saatchi, London
(AD) Carlos (CW) Keith Bickel (P) Nadav Kander**

Cultures unfamiliar with the term 'going for a slash'
will be even more perplexed by this inconvenient
treatment of the slash and purple silk theme of the
long-running and diverse campaign.

SMOKING CAUSES CANCER

Chief Medical   Officers' Warning
5 mg Tar   0.5 mg Nicotine

Volkswagen Jetta (A) BAM Advertising, Toronto (AD) Duncan Bruce (CW) Aubrey Singer (P) George Simhoni

We are talking here about heated windshield washer nozzles. What else?

It's a small thing, but ours are heated.

Heated windshield washer nozzles, we'd wager, are not high on the check-lists of most new car buyers. Small things. Mere details. In totally redesigning the Volkswagen Jetta, we recognized that a car is nothing more than many thousands of small details bound together. And any one can be made to make a car safer, faster or friendlier. On an unlit highway, some stormy night in February, the small heated nozzles that clean the wind screen on all new Volkswagen Jettas become perfect examples of the inspired attention small things receive from our engineers. Inspiration is commonplace on the Jetta. It's no surprise then, to learn Jetta has been designed with a superior steel safety cage and increased headroom, legroom, shoulder room, trunk room, and finely tuned engines that both accelerate and exhilarate. And so on. When test driving, you'll find few cars that recognize small things as big opportunities. And just one that makes the most of them.

THE NEW JETTA VW

Definitely not middle of the road.

**The British Council (A) Ogilvy & Mather, Singapore
(AD&P) Sally Overheu (CW) Jackie Mathiramani**

Improve your English. Or enjoy the consequences.

**Olympus Binoculars (A) Lowe Howard-Spink, London
(AD) Steve Dunn (CW) Tony Barry (P) Stock Shots**

The scientific term is about as inaccessible and
unwieldy as the original title of the company, named
after its founder Takachiho Seisakusho.

If there's one thing that annoys a dedicated ornithologist like yourself, it's the same old innuendoes about 'bird' watching. But hopefully, the binocular gift sets from Olympus will give you something to smile about.

Binoculars that are compact, lightweight and come with a twenty five year guarantee. A field list to keep a record of your sightings.

And in the unlikely event that you don't recognise what you've just seen, we have even included a pocket sized photographic guide book to the Birds of Britain and Europe.

All in all, we think you will agree that although some people may snigger when you mention your favourite hobby, Olympus take it all just a little bit more seriously.

OLYMPUS BINOCULARS
The complete bird watchers' gift set

We won't resort to cheap jokes about birds, boobies and tits. So here's a picture of the *Phalacrocorax aristotelis.*

A G Barr/ Irn-Bru (A) The Leith Agency, Edinburgh
(AD) Glenn Smith (CW) Craig Roderick (P) Hulton Deutch Collection

By adding quirky captions to archive photographs, innocuous images are converted into posters that reposition the product at the trendy end of the market.

**Abbot Ale (A) Delaney Fletcher Bozell,
London (AD) David Adamson
(CW) Richard Prentice (P) Mark Polyblank**

By becoming a monk in Bury St Edmunds
monastery 700 years ago you received
compensations for the life of celibacy -
eight pints of ale every evening.

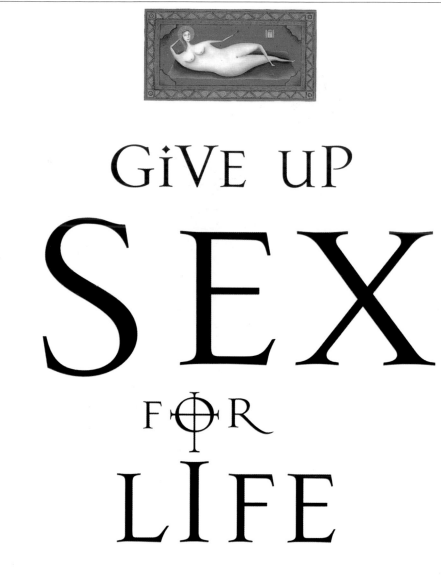

GiVE uP

SEX

FⓉR

LIFE

SEVEN hundred years ago life in the Bury St. Edmunds monastery wasn't exactly a laugh a minute. You got up at two in the morning and had breakfast twelve hours later.

In between there was an unending diet of prayer and chanting. Followed by more prayer and chanting.

Still it wasn't all bad news. Every evening you were allowed eight pints of

the Abbot's Ale. (Twelve if you were ill.)

It was brewed in the monastery's own brewery with natural spring water drawn from its own well.

Today we're still drawing water from the same source and still using local barley for our own Abbot Ale. Blessed by the Sabbath (fermented for

ABBOT ALE

a painstaking seven days to you), it has a rich, deep flavour.

There is one concession to the 20th Century however, it also comes in cans courtesy of a widget.

With so much practice, it's no surprise that many think it's one of the finest real ales you can buy.

It's almost worth giving up sex for. At least for a couple of hours.

Sweet & Nasty Boston (AD) Larry Bowdish (CW) Richard Swietek

Those with a deflated idea of their sexual prowess can discover the satisfaction shepherds have enjoyed for centuries.

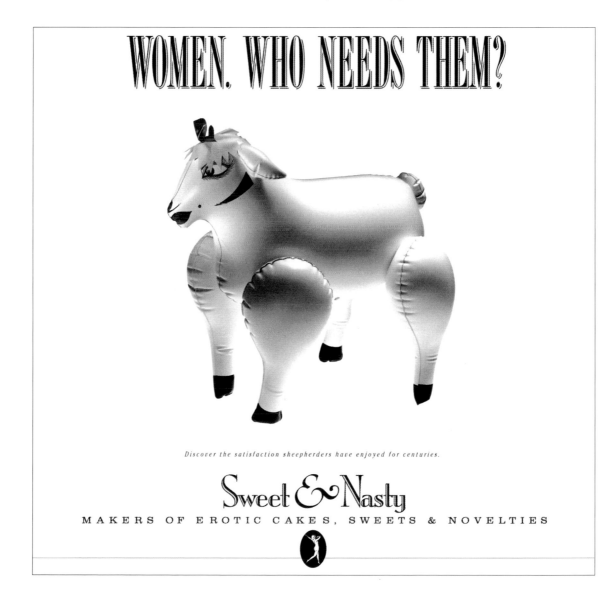

We don't guarantee custom

MISTER HAR

OVER 100 VARIETIES OF CONDO

Mister Hard Head (A) Birdsall-Voss & Kloppenburg,
Milwaukee (AD) Scott Krahn (CW) Gary Mueller
(P) Dick Baker

Humour sweetens the pill. And protects you from any
embarassment over sensitive or taboo subjects.

Moulin Rouge Cabaret Restaurant
(A) Hunt Lascaris TBWA, Cape Town
(CD) Stephen Burke (ADs) Neil Dawson,
Clint Bryce & Jenny McCartan
(CWs) Clive Pickering, Stephen Burke &
Jenny McCartan (P) Andrew Cole

Το Υπουργείο Υγ είας προειδοποιεί:
ΤΟ ΚΑΠΝΙΣΜΑ ΒΛΑΠΤΕΙ ΣΟΒΑΡΑ ΤΗΝ ΥΓΕΙΑ

Gallaher/Silk Cut (A) M & C Saatchi, London (AD) Carlos
(CW) Keith Bickel (P) Nitin Vadukul (Modelmaker) Nancy Fouts

Being a screw, the blatant phallic reference is doubly
appropriate. Turned down by the Advertising Standards
Authority, the purple centrefold only appeared in a Greek
Men's magazine.

Hyperbole

**Pan-Britannica Industries/Baby Bio (A) TBWA, London
(CD & CW) Trevor Beattie (AD) Steve Chetham**

How high can you go on hyperbole? Clearly, the sky's the limit.

We have wood fillers for any job around the house.

LePage (A) Kuleba & Shyllit, Toronto (AD) Joe Shyllit (CW) Jerry Kuleba (P) George Simhoni

Whether or not you find something funny depends on how seriously you take it. View this Tom-and-Jerry style scene as ridiculous, and everyone's happy.

Not all holes are created equal. That's why LePage, the Adhesive Experts, makes a whole range of wood fillers for indoors and out. From versatile "Plastic Wood®" to handy tinted wood fillers to practical wood fillers that can brave the elements outdoors. And once applied, LePage wood fillers stay on the job without shrinking or cracking. Plus you can treat them like wood. They are easy to stain and can be sawed, drilled, cut, nailed, and screwed. So regardless of how the hole got there, take comfort in knowing LePage has the best range of wood fillers for the job.

LEPAGE
Stick with the best.

Available at: Beaver Lumber, Canadian Tire, Do-It Centres, Home Depot, Home Hardware, Pro Hardware, Revelstoke Home Centres, and True Value Hardware

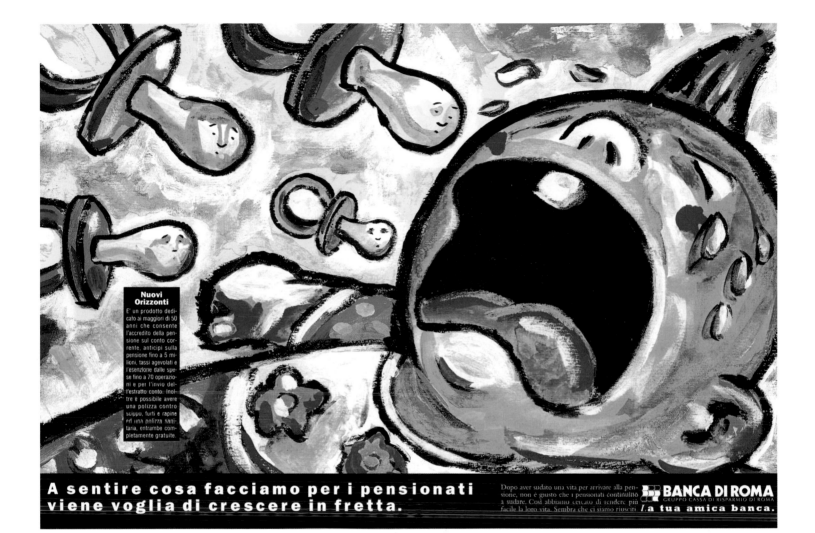

Banca di Roma (A) Saatchi & Saatchi, Rome
(CDs) Stefano Maria Palombi & Luca Albanese (AD) Luca Albanese
(CW) Stefano Maria Palombi (Illustrator) Alberto Ruggieri

This ad introduces bank facilities and services for the over
fifties with the line: 'If you hear what we are doing for retired
people, you will be eager to grow old quickly.'

Lee Jeans (A) Fallon McElligott,
Minneapolis (AD) Arty Tan (CW) Mike Gibbs
(P) Shawn Michienzi Mavvy Studio

Lee Lites. A new line of lightweight denim.

Light, cool comfortable jeans with a remarkably soft hand. Perfect for all seasons. Available in two different finishes: Aged Stone and Aged Blue. Call your Lee sales representative today. Because Lee Lites are just what the market ordered. And they just might take off without you.

The Sugar Huts (A) Ogilvy & Mather, Singapore (AD/Typographer) Thomas Low (CW) Steve Elrick (Illustrators) Bok/David Chin

If you don't find the ad amusing, you're probably not the sort of person who'd enjoy The Sugar Hut.

More relaxed

than an extremely chilled-out

chemically laid-back hippy

floating in a sensory deprivation tank

in the middle of a rain forest,

during a valium-induced coma.

On a Sunday.

The Sugar Huts, scattered about in acres of flower-filled gardens, with three swimming-pools to choose from, and air-con, and mini-bars, and room-service, and the best Thai restaurant in town, or rather, out-of-town, near Pattaya, just off the road to Jomtien Beach. Call (038) 251686.

Pizza World (A) Delvico Bates, Barcelona (ADs) David Caballero and Lucho Correa (CW) Toni Segarra (P) Ramon Serrano

Humour often works selectively. If you feel positive about a brand or a subject, the humour will work. If not, it won't.

**Aftershock (A) Fallon McElligott, Minneapolis
(AD) Nic York (CW) Eric Sorenson
(P and illustrator) Gerry Bybee**

Visual hyperbole - the most effective way of
illustrating/conveying feeling, taste or smell
which cannot be seen.

X.O. Beer (A) Ogilvy & Mather, Singapore
(CD, AD & CW) Neil French (P) Hanchew

The businessman's equivalent of the lager lout is older, but not necessarily wiser.

Branding

Senna Import/Audi A8 (A) ALMAP/BBDO,
Sao Paulo (AD) Marcello Serpa
(CWs) Ricardo Amaral (Chester) & Atila
Francucci (P) Mauricio Nahas

The Audi A8 - the first car to be made
of recyclable aluminium.

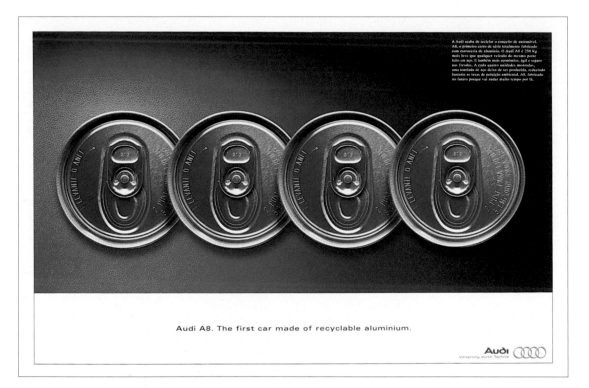

The Economist (A) Abbott Mead Vickers BBDO, London
(CD) David Abbott (AD) Paul Briginshaw
(CW) Malcolm Duffy (Typographer) Joe Hoza

When the public recognizes your logo, style or colour, the value of the communication is doubled. Combine this instant recognition with a style of wit that resonates with the target market and you're up there with the leaders.

The Economist

Blunt, yet sharp.

The Economist

Top desk publishing.

The Economist

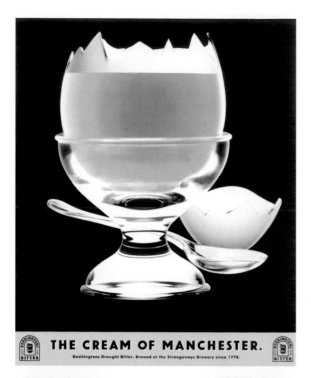

**Whitbread/Boddingtons (A) Bartle Bogle
Hegarty, London (CD) John Hegarty
(AD) Graham Watson (CW) Bruce Crouch
(P) Tif Hunter**

The Cream of Manchester campaign
transformed a relatively small, regional
brand of beer into a leading national bitter.
It succeeds by virtue of its simplicity and
consistency, focusing single-mindedly on
the product attributes - its creamy head
and golden colour.

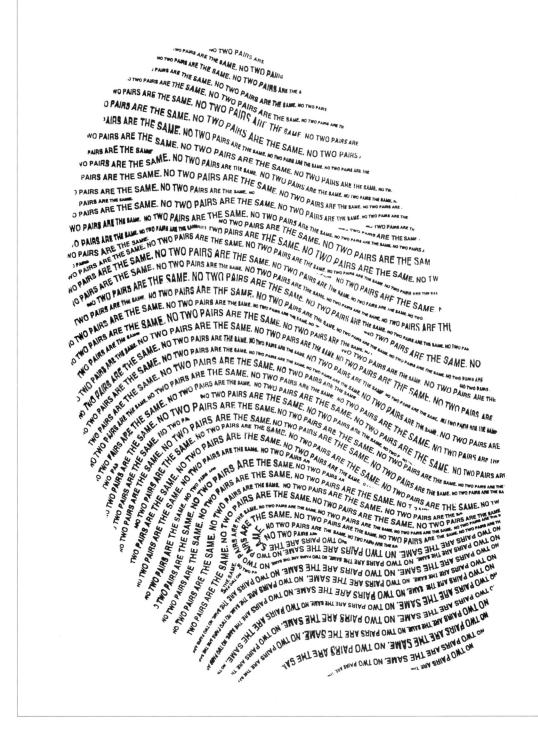

Levi Strauss/Red Tab (A) Bartle Bogle Hegarty, London (CD) John Hegarty (AD) Graham Watson (CW) Bruce Crouch (Typographer) Sid Russell

There are jeans and jeans and jeans. And then there are Levi jeans. The name itself is synonymous with jeans. Not only are they durable, they're unique. As a thumbprint. Not just distinct from the competition, but each pair is distinctive! And, just how personal can you get? For your own Personal Pair of Levis your measurements can be tapped into a computer and the bespoke jeans delivered to your doorstep.

Sophisticated Hush Puppies.

Our classic pumps. For those with a nose for the finer things.

**Wolverine/Hush Puppies (A) Fallon
McElligott, Minneapolis (AD) Bob Barrie
(CW) Jarl Olsen (P) Rick Dublin**

With a simple, one-word translation,
the corporate symbol - the Basset Hound
- has been used around the world.

Perrier Vittel UK (A) Publicis, London
(AD) Rick Ward (CW) Noel Sharman (P) Adrian Burke

Pun and Games

Triumph International (A) Delaney Fletcher Bozell, London
(CDs) Greg Delaney/Brian Stewart (AD) Brian Stewart
(CW) Greg Delaney (P) Pamela Hanson, represented by Fiona
Cowan/Hamiltons Photographers Ltd

£19.99 'Order' suede retro trainer in red, black or navy *Clarks*

Clark's Shoes (A) TBWA, London
(AD) Chris Hodgkiss (CW) Pip Bishop
(P) Joseph Hunwick

THE PERFECT SHOES
FOR NEXT TO NOTHING.

THE CLASSIC LOAFER £29·99 ONLY AVAILABLE FROM
Clarks

Clark's Shoes (A) McCann Erickson,
Manchester (AD) David Price
(CW) Zak Mroueh (P) David Stewart

**Caffrey's Irish ale (A) WCRS, London (AD) Andy Dibb
(CW) Giles Davis (P) Max Forsythe (Typographer) Barry Brand**

Armagh is looking good. She's full of down-to-earth, heart-of-
gold, honest-to-goodness realism, with the essence of Irish
blarney beneath the raw exterior.

Whitbread/Murphy's (A) Bartle Bogle Hegarty, London (CD) John Hegarty (AD) Graham Watson (CW) Bruce Crouch (P) Mike Parsons (Illustrator) Sara Hodge

Eugene inherited his Uncle Clancy's estate, but like the Murphy's he wasn't bitter.

Mattel Scrabble Challenge
(A) Ogilvy & Mather, Singapore
(CD) Steve Elrick (AD) Thomas Low
(CW) Graham Kelly

**Axel Springer Verlag/Bild Zeitung
(A) Jung von Matt, Hamburg (CD) Thilo von
Büren (AD) Daniela Sautter (CW) Stefan Meske**

There is a newspaper without nonsense.
TGIF...thank goodness it's funny.

Selfridges (A) Saatchi & Saatchi, London
(CD) Adam Kean (AD) Viv Walsh (CW) Jo Tanner
(P) Hans Gissenger (Typographer) Paul Beer

Images from a real airport x-ray machine were used to
promote the new Selfridges store at Heathrow airport.

SELFRIDGES *now* INSPIRES
flyers'
DESIRES *at* HEATHROW *terminal* ONE.

Switch Card Services (A) Collett Dickenson Pearce, London (CDs) Guy Moore/Tony Malcolm (AD) Phil Forster (CW) Michael Burke (P) Tim O'Sullivan, represented by Andrea Rosenberg (Modelmaker) Ron Mueck

You seldom need dough nowadays.

Stella Artois (A) Lowe Howard-Spink, London
(AD) Simon Butler (CW) Gethin Stout (P) Sebastian Kruger

Imagine you're juggling with the words Cash and Czech, then stumble on this interpretation of American Express. It serves well and gives you the advantage.

Imperial Tobacco/Regal Cigarettes (A) Lowe Howard-Spink,
London (CD) Adrian Holmes (AD) Simon Morris (CW) Jeff Smith
(P) Tim O'Sullivan, represented by Andrea Rosenberg

Find the character's name within the brand. What personality
does that name suggest? Train spotting? Then take the term
literally, and his response is to say: 'There's one!'

Decorative tea service, circa 1760.

Made in silver.

Made in England.

Maid in torment.

Indian. China. Earl Grey. What comes out of this tea service is nothing compared to what has gone into it. Handmade by Asprey, it's a reproduction of a John Swift design and is available in our showrooms along with other exquisite silverware. Our profound apologies to maids everywhere.

Asprey
LONDON

**Asprey (A) M & C Saatchi, London (AD) Gary Marshall
(CW) Paul Marshall (P) Helmut Newton, represented by Tiggy
Maconochie/ Hamiltons Photographers Ltd**

The strategy was to produce upmarket yet quirky ads,
giving the brand a distinctive tone. This was achieved by
using 'staff' to send up the whole concept.

Sony Portable Radio (A) Tokyo Agency International, Tokyo
(CD) Masayuki Takayama (AD) Toshiro Fumizono
(CW) Noriaki Hida (P) Masao Torii

When the game ends, the cord disappears - in Japanese
literally 'gets put away'. The subhead reads: 'The radio that
lets you put away the long cord when you aren't listening'.

In Japanese the words for end and put away have the same
sound on the first syllable, creating a subtle play on words.

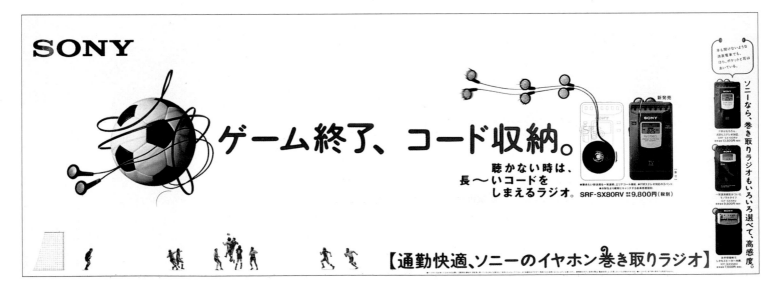

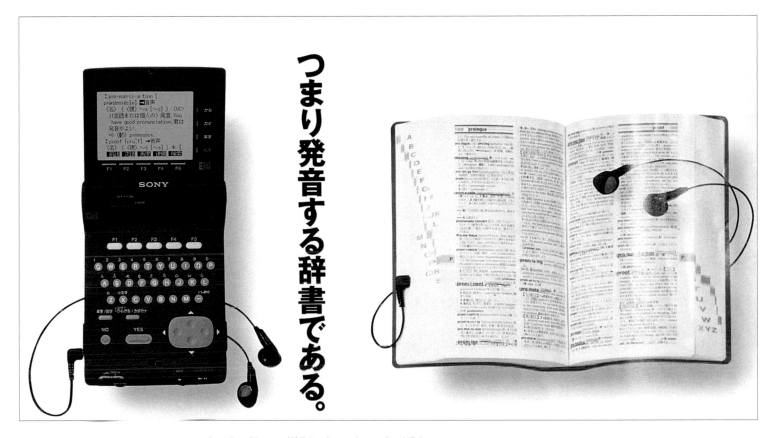

つまり発音する辞書である。

Sony Data Discman **(A)** Tokyo Agency International, Tokyo
(CD) Naoki Murakami **(AD)** Masaaki Akita **(CW)** Hirofumi Mochinaga
(P) Shunsuke Mizoe

A dictionary that pronounces the words for you. Subhead:
'With an electronic dictionary you can look up the sound too'.
The Japanese verb hiberu (be able to look up) is not normally
used in this context - to look up a sound. It is used for 'look up
a word in a dictionary', so the play on words gets across the
idea that the Data Discman is a talking 'dictionary' and you
can look up sounds too.

**Time Magazine (A) Fallon McElligott,
Minneapolis (AD) Bob Barrie
(CW) Dean Buckhorn (P) Christopher Morris**

There's more to this ad than the pun on
burying people. The tag line that runs with
all the ads in the campaign rings true:
Understanding comes with TIME. It sounds
like an established axiom which supports
the assertion that the magazine gives
thorough coverage of issues that matter.

People who are willing to die
for freedom shouldn't be buried
in the middle of the newspaper.

Understanding comes with TIME.

Teijin (A) Tokyo Agency International, Tokyo
(CDs) Naoki Murakami/Masaaki Akita/Shunichi
Iwasaaki (ADs) Masaaki Akita/Takashi Sano
(CW) Shinji Tao

Teijin, the people that make people happy.
Subhead: 'Teijin is always on the move. For
you. For the people you love'.
A play on the Japanese words ningen (people)
and teijin (the name of the company), because
when written in Japanese, both words use the
letter for 'person', reinforcing the assertion:
We are a very human company.

Cruel Humour

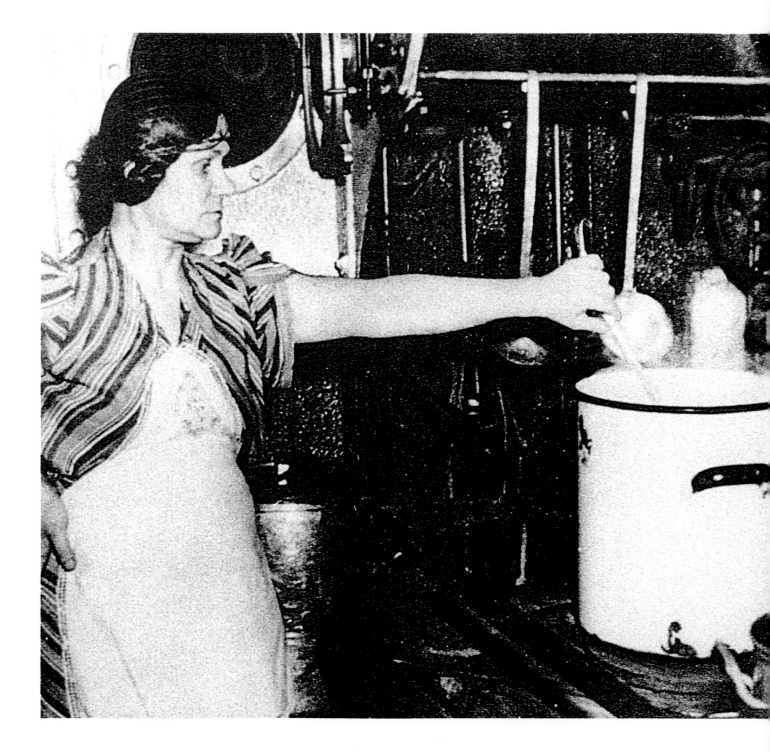

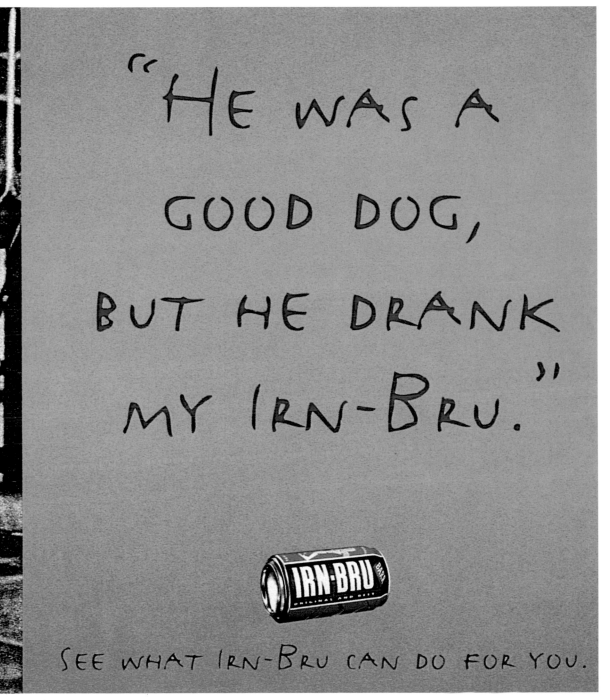

A G Barr/Irn-Bru (A) The Leith Agency, Edinburgh (AD) Gareth Howells (CW) Dougal Wilson (P) Hulton Deutch Collection

What seemed hilariously funny when I was younger, now seems heartless. And what I viewed as peculiar, I now split my sides over.

Nissan Micra (A) TBWA, London
(AD) Chris Hodgkiss (CW) Pip Bishop (P) John Claridge

BLUE CAN WARNING.

IF THE CAN TURNS BLUE THE COLA'S GONE FLAT.

Brussels directive E-3240 B outlaws the sale of cola after its "best before" date.

Thanks to new developments in packaging technology, in the unlikely event of a can of Virgin Cola remaining unsold after the statutory period, the can will react with the cola and turn blue.

Virgin strongly advises its customers to avoid <u>all</u> blue cans of cola. They are clearly out of date.

Virgin Cola (A) Rainey Kelly Campbell Roalfe, London (AD/CW) Derek Payne/Mark Roalfe

Ads that knock competitors usually do so with a blunt instrument. Virgin Cola's blue can was a wickedly adroit April Fool that appeared just before Pepsi's multi-million dollar change to blue livery in April 1996.

**Wall Street Boxing (A) Hill Holliday
Connors Cosmopulos, Boston
(CD) Fred Bertino (ADs) Tim Foley/Mike
Plato (CW) Marty Donohue
(Ps) Cheryl Dunn/Jeff Coolidge (Illustrator)
Roger Andrews**

The punchy, in yer face ad appeals to the
simmering cravings of the urban stressed,
offering both highly paid stockbrokers
and lowly traders an authentic and legal
way to vent their aggression.

**Jonathan Sceats Sunglasses (A) BAM/SSB, Sydney
(AD) Darryn Devlin (CW) Bobbi Gassy (P) Michael Corridore**

Cruel? Disrespectful? Bad Taste? The target market wouldn't
be seen dead responding to any other strategy. The simulated
stiff was shot at Saint Vincent's Hospital morgue, alongside 17
genuinely dead bodies.

Don't be seen dead in anything else. Jonathan Sceats Sunglasses.

GASP (Group Against Smoking Pollution) (A) Houston, Herstate, Farat (AD) Larry Bowdish (CW) Roger Baldacci (P) Russ Quackenbush

Sometimes, belligerent humour is the only legal weapon left when faced with the might of large corporations with transparent vested interests.

THE TOBACCO COMPANIES SAY THAT SMOKING WILL MAKE YOU MORE ATTRACTIVE. THEN AGAIN, LOOK WHO RUNS THE TOBACCO COMPANIES.

GASP

Future Exxon Ship Captain In Training.

**Blackhawk Farms Off-Road Challenge
(A) BVK/McDonald (AD) Scott Krahn,
Milwaukee (CW) Gary Mueller (P) Stock**

Jokes at someone's expense find more
favour if a consensus believes the victim
deserves it.

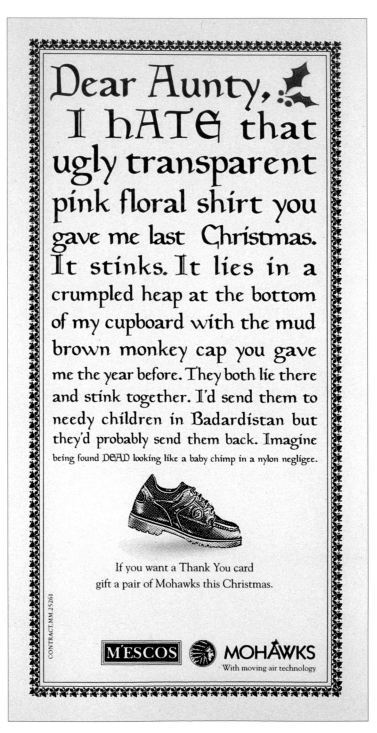

Mohawks (A) Contract Advertising, New Delhi (AD) Sonja Aggarwal (CW) Vidur Vohra

Christmas letters will never be the same again.

For 8 free mini Tampax, write to Barbara Lee, Tambrands Ltd. (Dept Y55), PO Box 1020, Llangollen LL20 8YZ. Or for Ireland, Tambrands Ireland Ltd (Dept Y55), Rosanna Road, Tipperary.

NAME

ADDRESS

POSTCODE

DATE OF BIRTH

WHAT DO YOU USE?
☐ TAMPONS   ☐ TOWELS   ☐ PANTLINERS

WHICH BRAND DO YOU
USE MOST OFTEN?

Of course you have loads of things in your life other than boys, like er,......... well OK, like clothes for instance.

And isn't it nice just occasionally to wear that dress that isn't just drop-dead gorgeous but more drop-dead-roll-over-bite-the-furniture-and-drool-like-a-pathetic-dog gorgeous?

Let's be clear what we're talking about here.

It's the kind of dress you need attitude to wear.

It's the kind of dress you may even need a padded bra to wear.

And it's the kind of dress that you definitely do not need a towel to wear.

The trouble is, that party that HE is definitely going to be at and where HE will be knocked out by the sheer power of your sex appeal and HE will finally become putty in your hands, is on the same day that IT arrives.

Your period. With its impeccable sense of timing.

Tampax tampons are made for this kind of thing. Because you don't have to feel one jot less confident when you have your period than when you don't.

And no matter how short your skirt or how tight your PVC, no one will

have a clue that it's anything other than a normal day of the month.

Tampax tampons thoughtfully come in four absorbencies to suit the various different stages of your period.

There are higher absorbencies for your heavier days, and mini ones for those lighter days.

So you can feel perfectly confident there's no danger of leaking.

And don't worry about inserting it correctly. The applicator always places the tampon in exactly the right place inside you. So you won't be able to feel or see a thing.

Although there's nothing more natural than your period, there are times when there is nothing more uncomfortable.

Tampons aren't about making your period disappear; they just stop it dictating what you have to wear and when you have to wear it.

After all, who says that just because you are having your period, you stop being

TAMPAX®
Tampons

attractive to boys? Certainly not boys.

But you don't have to just take our word for it.

If you fill out the coupon at the top of the page and send it to us, we'll send you some free samples. In plenty of time for your next party.

Then you can get on with what you do best.

Inflicting some really serious damage on those floorboards.

just because i'm having my period, it doesn't stop me enjoying the sound of a chin hitting the floor.

Tambrands/Tampax (A) Abbott Mead Vickers BBDO, London (CD) David Abbott (AD) Damon Collins (CW) Mary Wear

FORGET YOUR

BUT FIRST CALL PETER DREFS. HE'S A MUSICIANS INSTITUTE HONORS GRADUATE AND NATIONALLY RECOGNIZED

SISTER'S HEAD,

DRUMMER. TO SET UP A CUSTOM SESSION, JUST CALL 414-728-6567. THEN HIT THE DRUMS. AFTER ALL,

BEAT ON THIS.

THEY'RE SMALL, ROUND AND HOLLOW. JUST LIKE YOUR SISTER'S HEAD.

Studio Cymbolizm (A) BVK/McDonald, Milwaukee (AD) Mike Ancevic (CW) Gary Mueller

Sadistic humour is a cruel tool in the armoury of aggressive advertising.

Mild Smiles

Triumph International (A) Delaney Fletcher
Bozell, London (AD) Steve Donoghue
(CW) John Peake (Illustrator) Claire Bretécher

ANY BRA WILL FIT YOU AT A PINCH.

Buying a bra couldn't be easier, could it?

Choose the style you like best and pick your size off the shelf.

Easy.

But what if it feels a little tighter than last time? Do you grin and bear it? Or take it back?

Finding a bra that will always feel as good as it looks is a lot easier than you might think.

Next time you buy a bra, try on a Triumph and you'll see what we mean.

We know that no two women are the same shape even when they're supposed to be the same size.

We've dozens of beautiful bras for you to choose from, each carefully tailored to the precise cup size.

So once you've found your size in a Triumph

Visuelle

bra, whatever style you choose, you're sure of a perfect fit every time.

And you won't have to pinch yourself to see if you're dreaming.

TRIUMPH HAS THE BRA FOR THE WAY YOU ARE.

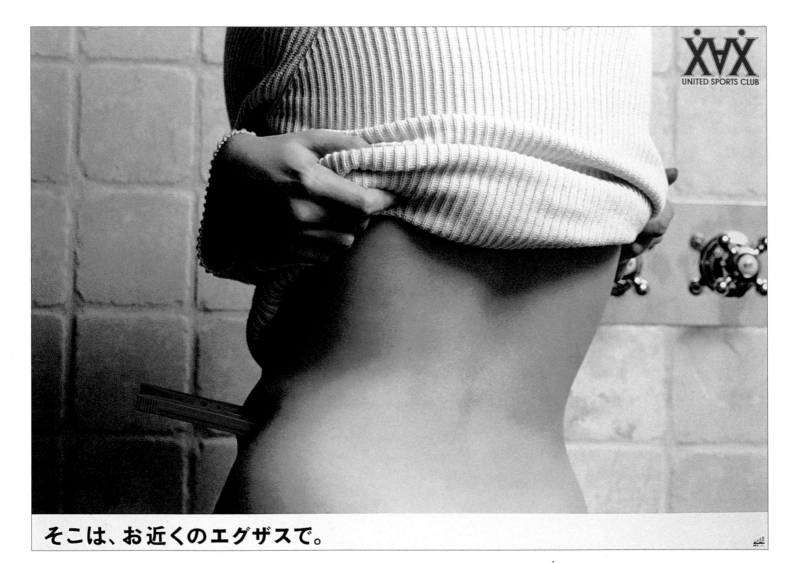

そこは、お近くのエグザスで。

XAX Athletic Club (A) McCann Erickson, Tokyo
(AD) Satoshi Kato (CW) Toshiya Mizoguchi (P) Shintaro Shiratori

Come to XAX for that part.

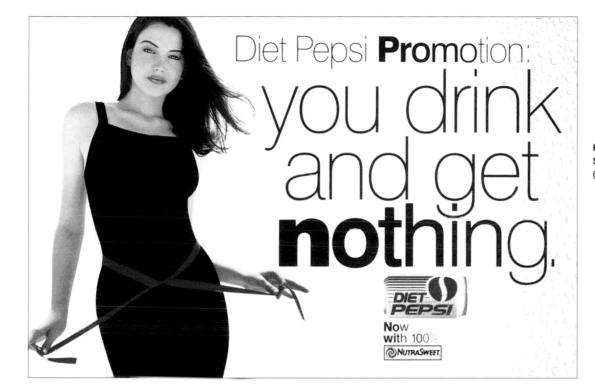

Pepsico & Cia/Diet Pepsi (A) ALMAP/BBDO, Sao Paulo (AD/CW) Marcello Serpa (Ps) J.R.Duran & Cassio Vasconcellos

Meat Products (A) TBWA/Campaign Company,
Amsterdam (AD) Diederick Hillenius
(CW) Lysbeth Bijlstra (P) Hans Kroeskamp

An irresistible temptation.

Lipton had squeezed every bit of real milk goodness into their superior tasting Lipton Plus Milk Tea.

Lipton

LIPTON PLUS MILK TEA.
The superior tasting tea. Now with real dairy milk.

Lipton Plus Milk Tea (A) Ogilvy & Mather, Singapore
(AD) Thomas Low (CW) Steve Elrick (Illustrator) David Chin

This all-in-one tea mix changed from using a non-dairy creamer to real milk. Naturally, cows were desperate to have the privilege of being chosen by the Lipton Plus people.

Amy and the girls heard the Lipton Plus people were searching for only the freshest milk.

LIPTON PLUS MILK TEA.
The superior tasting tea. Now with real dairy milk.

Friends of Public Education
(A) Fallon McElligott, Minneapolis
(AD) Ellen Steinberg (CW) Tom Rosen
(P) Stock

What is it in us that enjoys laughing at other people's mistakes? Sometimes we can excuse our cruel sense of humour by claiming that we are not laughing at them, but with them. But do we believe they are foolish or just their actions?

Stay in school.

Siglo XXI Newspaper (A) Leo Burnett,
Guatemala City (AD) Fernando Alegria
(CW) Estuardo Juarez

Come *potete* vedere, sul *Bali* 100
si *può andare* anche in *due.*

*I colori
sono belli belli,
la sella
è comoda comoda,
il motore
potente potente.
E voi
vi sentirete
leggeri leggeri.*

HONDA
*SJ*100 *Bali*

**Honda Motorcycles (A) Saatchi & Saatchi,
Rome (CDs) Stefano Maria Palombi/Luca
Albanese (AD) Grazia Cecconi (CW) Stefano
Maria Palombi (P) Marco Biondi**

As you can see, on a Bali 100 there's
enough room for two.

Metro Toronto Zoo (A) TBWA Chiat/Day,
Toronto (AD) Stephanie Owens
(CWs) Patti Maxim & Tim Tobias

**Two Oceans Aquarium (A) Hunt Lascaris TBWA, Cape Town
(CD) Stephen Burke (AD) Neil Dawson (CW) Clive Pickering**

This message appeared on one of Cape Town's most
popular beaches for the launch of a new aquarium on the
city's waterfront.

Out of Context

**Brooklyn Bagels (A) Ogilvy & Mather, Singapore
(AD) Thomas Low (CW) Steve Elrick**

When a group of young American entrepreneurs
imported genuine bagel ovens from New York, along
with their mothers'traditional Yiddish recipe, the local
Chinese population just had to react.

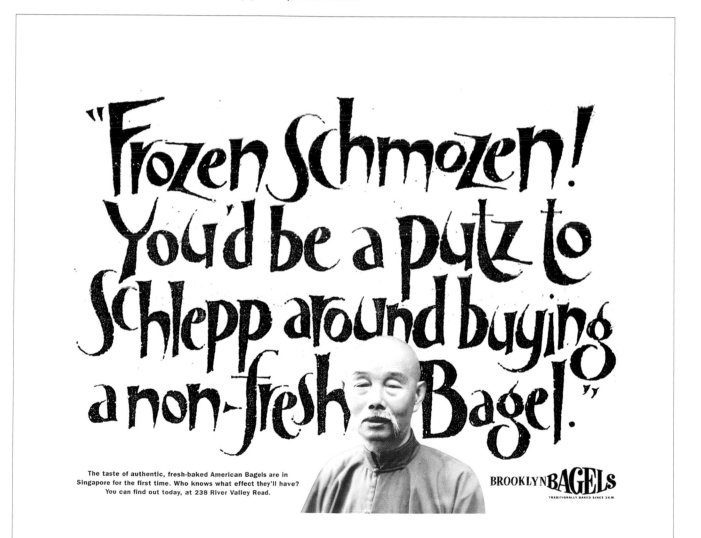

"Frozen Schmozen! You'd be a putz to schlepp around buying a non-fresh Bagel."

The taste of authentic, fresh-baked American Bagels are in
Singapore for the first time. Who knows what effect they'll have?
You can find out today, at 238 River Valley Road.

BROOKLYN BAGELS
TRADITIONALLY BAKED SINCE 3 A.M.

Wickes (A) Lowe Howard-Spink, London
(AD) Kevin Thomas (CW) John Silver

Inside the squat, Ringwood and Sergeant Boyle made straight for the bathroom.

A zit-faced, shaven-headed youth was desperately trying to flush the toilet.

Ringwood stared down the pan, where a plastic bag of marijuana was obstinately floating. He glared at the youth.

"You make me sick, you lot. No morals. No manners. No self-respect. But you know what really gets me? It's your totally inadequate waste-disposal systems."

He pressed the flush lever. The cistern gurgled emptily.

"This thing needs a new ballvalve. £3.99 at Wickes. Or better still, get a new white china cistern for £51.99.

Nick him, Sergeant."

If home improvement's your religion, worship at ▼ Wickes

96

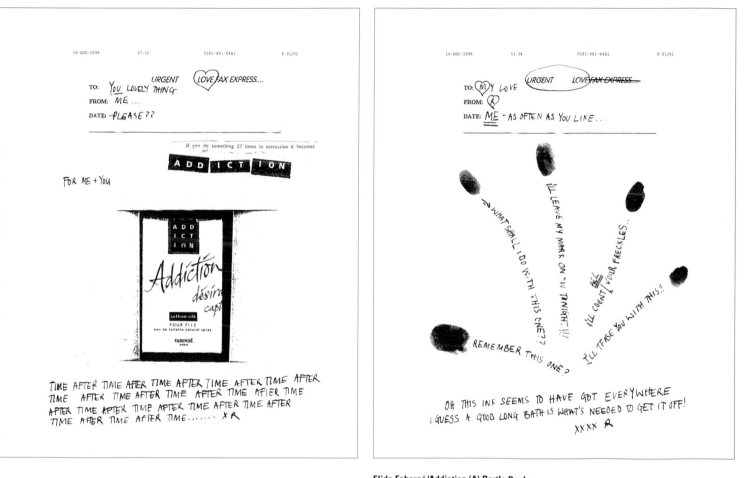

Elida Fabergé/Addiction (A) Bartle Bogle
Hegarty, London (CD) Dennis Lewis (Concept
creator/AD/CW/ Illustrator) Martin Galton
(AD/CW/Illustrator) Elvis Robertson
(CW) Will Awdry (Typographer) Andy Bird

Your inquisitive colleagues are going to be
intrigued by your heaven-scent faxes. But,
at least someone has changed the
predictable fragrance of perfume ads. Fax
like this make scents.

Gallaher/Benson & Hedges
(A) Collett Dickenson Pearce, London
(AD) Tina Morgan (P) John Hammond

Rocks from Lyme Regis on England's
South Coast were arranged with fossils
from a shop and sprinkled with a dusting
of sand and aluminium powder.

MIDDLE TAR As defined by H.M. Government
DANGER: H.M. Government Health Departments' WARNING: THINK ABOUT THE HEALTH RISKS BEFORE SMOKING

Swatch (A) Barbella Gagliardi Saffirio, Milan (CD) Pasquale Barbella (AD) Manuela Colombo (CW) Laura Colombo (P) Hermes Carli

Swatch makes sense ... even if the cave painting doesn't.

Swatch (A) Barbella Gagliardi Saffirio, Milan
(CD) Pasquale Barbella (AD) Manuela Colombo
(CW) Laura Colombo (P) Hermes Carl

Lindsay Kemp - dancer, mime and choreographer
- created the first Swatch dedicated to dance.
The flamboyant motifs superimpose a character
onto the watches, which come to life in a well-
timed dance routine.

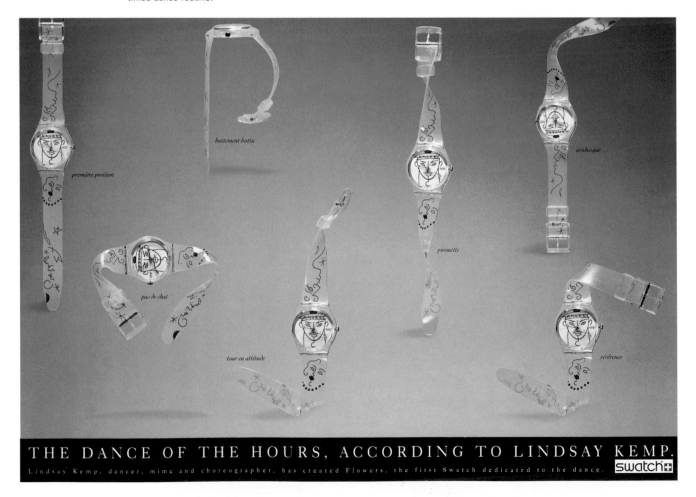

THE DANCE OF THE HOURS, ACCORDING TO LINDSAY KEMP.

Lindsay Kemp, dancer, mime and choreographer, has created Flowers, the first Swatch dedicated to the dance.

swatch✛

Messe Frankfurt/Interstoff
(A) R.G. Wiesmeier, Munich
(CDS) Claudia Hammerschmidt & Hajo
Depper (AD) Sabine Hohring
(CW) Hajo Depper (P) Stock

Where in the world can you get the most beautiful fabrics? If you can't get them here, you can get them there. At the new Interstoff International Fabric and Accessories show.

So you don't believe there are any new accessories? Don't believe. Look. At the new Interstoff.

The Unexpected

UNITED COLORS
OF BENETTON.

Benetton (A) In-house, Italy (AD/P) Oliviero Toscani

Never kiss-off the element of surprise. She should have expected the unexpected.

Gallaher/Benson & Hedges
(A) Collett Dickenson Pearce, London
(AD) Paul Briginshaw (P) Barry Lategan

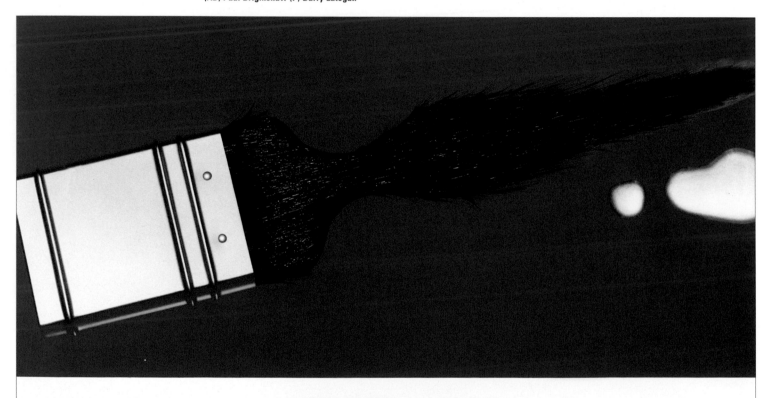

MIDDLE TAR As defined by H.M.Government
Warning: SMOKING CAN CAUSE HEART DISEASE Health Departments' Chief Medical Officers

MIDDLE TAR As defined by H.M. Government
I. M. Government Health Departments' WARNING: THINK ABOUT THE HEALTH RISKS BEFORE SMOKING

Gallaher/Benson & Hedges (A) Collett Dickenson Pearce, London (AD) Nigel Rose (P) Max Forsythe

Visual gymnastics leave half the population feeling smug and the rest perplexed. Like transferred epithets, they're surreally intriguing. Intrigue attracts our attention like a magnet and then, having mastered the mystery we attach greater value to the product... or at least the advertising.

Kodak Gold film (A) Advico Young & Rubican, Zurich

ZEREAU DEGREES

Perrier Vittel UK (A) Publicis, London
(AD) Rick Ward (CW) Noel Sharman
(P) Paul Bevitt (Modelmaker) Tim Weare & Partners

If we smile, the advertiser is happy.

Audi S6 (A) Bartle Bogle Hegarty, London
(CD) John Hegarty (AD) Andrew Smart
(CW) Roger Beckett (P) Russell Porcas
(Typographer) Jeff Merrells

Disclaimer:
Audi cannot accept responsibility for those drivers who believe they can handle the 230bhp Audi S6 only to discover they are disturbed by its ability to accelerate from 0-60 in 6.7 seconds. Please think carefully before purchasing a car of this calibre.

Audi
Vorsprung durch Technik

Agency Staff Recruitment
(A) Hill Holliday Connors Cosmopulos, Boston

Agency promotion (A) New Deal, Oslo

The client asked 'What time is it?'. I replied 'What would you like it to be?'

Pattaya Paintball Park
(A) Ogilvy & Mather, Singapore
(AD & P) Thomas Low (CW) Steve Elrick

Some people release tension by kicking
a ball around a muddy field. Others play
music loudly. Others shoot plastic paint
pellets at the opposition.

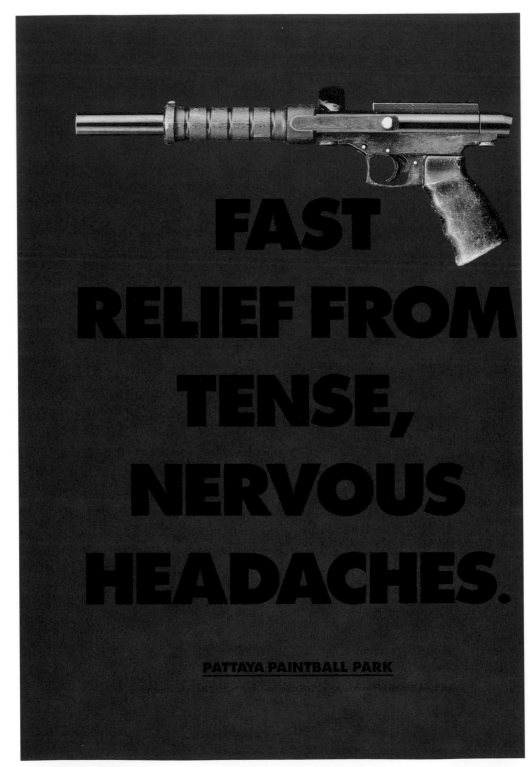

Dainfern Country Club (A) Hunt Lascaris TBWA, Cape Town (CD) Stephen Burke (AD/CW) Neil Dawson/Clive Pickering (P) Martyn Taylor

If divot trimming is your speciality, you'll relate to this invitation to turn the game into child's play.

Look At It Another Way

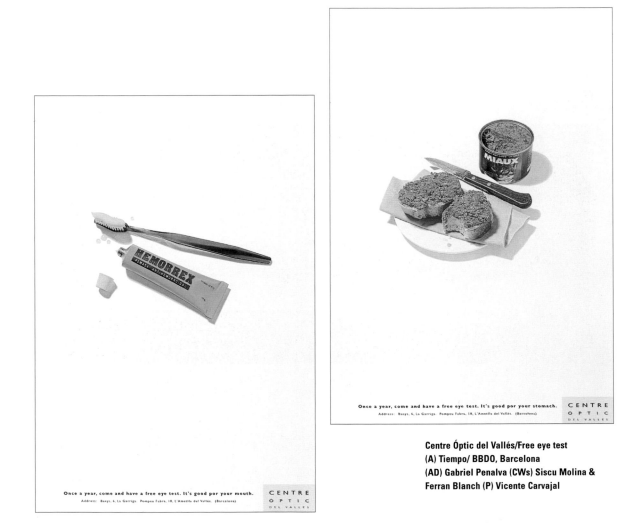

Centre Óptic del Vallés/Free eye test
(A) Tiempo/ BBDO, Barcelona
(AD) Gabriel Penalva (CWs) Siscu Molina &
Ferran Blanch (P) Vicente Carvajal

Opticians (A) TBWA/Campaign Company,
Amsterdam (AD) Diederick Hillonius
(CW) Lysbeth Bijlstra (P) Paul Ruigrok

So. Isn't it time you saw an optician?

Smirnoff (A) Lowe Howard-Spink, London
(AD) David Christensen (CW) Simon Carbery
(P) David Scheinman

Smirnoff (A) Lowe Howard-Spink, London
(AD) Simon Butler (CW) Gethin Stout (P) Paul Wakefield

Smithkline Beecham/Panadol (A) Tiempo/ BBDO,
Barcelona (AD) Gabriel Penalva (CWs) Siscu Molina &
Ferran Blanch

Study the problem carefully. Then consider the cure.

THE PARAKEET CAGE.

In the cage all parakeets are blue, but two. All are yellow, but two. All are green, but two. How many parakeets are there of each colour?

EINSTEIN AND HIS STUDENTS.

Half his students study trigonometry. A fourth part study physics and a seventh part read a book. Besides, three of them have not come to class today. How many students are there in Einstein's class?

PETER'S FRIENDS.

Peter has two friends: Anthony and David. Peter is two years older than David and Anthony is eight years younger. Their three ages add up to 50 years. How old are they?

BACK TO THE FUTURE.

Gabriel was 39 years old in 1990, but only 34 in 1995. How is that possible?

Momentum Life (A) Hunt Lascaris TBWA,
Cape Town (CD) Tony Granger
(AD) Erich Funke (CW) Wendy Moorcroft
(Illustrator) Lise Holloway

René Lezard (A) Jung von Matt, Hamburg
(CD) Deneke von Weltzien (AD) Lars Kruse
(CW) Stefan Meske (P) Kajetan Kandler

Always dress well. For everyone will be
reborn the way he has lived.

Autogerma S.p.A./Audi A6 TDI Quattro
(A) Verba DDB, Milan (CD/AD) Gianfranco
Marabelli (CD/CW) Enrico Bonomini
(P) Carlo Paggiarino

Hush Puppies (A) Young & Rubicam, London (P) Elliott Erwitt/Magnum

ACKNOWLEDGMENTS

My thanks to all the humourously creative creatives whose work appears in this book. And to their PAs, secretaries and agents, as well as the art buyers and account handlers, who helped process the paperwork. Not forgetting the clients who commissioned the work in the first place.

My special thanks also go to Fran, Gromit, Penny Foulkes, Bob Prior, Tim Rich, Philip Spink and Wallace. To Claudia and Daniel for interior and jacket design respectively. And to Richard Reynolds, whose velvet-coated brickbats have grown wings.

INDEX

Nissan Micra (A) TBWA, London
(AD) Chris Hodgkiss (CW) Pip Bishop (P) John Claridge

128